This book
belongs to:

....

MY FIRST
HOR

INGRID ANDE

ILLUSTRATIONS BY LEI

PHOTOGRAPHY BY MARIE PAUL

SKYHORSE PUBLISHING

MY FIRST BOOK OF
HORSES

INGRID ANDERSSON

ILLUSTRATIONS BY LENA FURBERG

PHOTOGRAPHY BY MARIE PAULSSON-BERTMAR

SKYHORSE PUBLISHING

This book
belongs to:

....

Contents

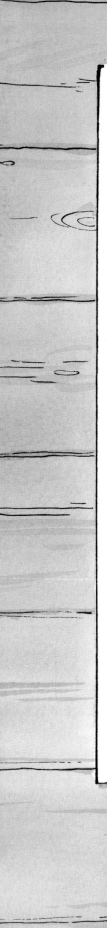

Horses—the best in the world!

Horses are beautiful animals! They are quick, strong, and graceful. They also have soft fur and are silky around the muzzle.

Maybe you have met a horse before at riding school, the races, or during a pony ride. If you have, then you already know that horses can range in size, from huge work horses to very small ponies.

The history of horses

Five thousand years ago, all horses were wild and free. They lived in small herds, with about ten to fifteen horses in each group.

Wild horses roamed the land and spent most of their time eating grass. They knew which grasses and plants were good to eat, and knew how to survive outside in all kinds of weather. When it rained, the herd would gather with their backsides to the rain, put their heads down, and huddle together to keep themselves warm.

When it was hot during the summer, they would roll in clay to protect themselves from the flies, mosquitos, and the sun's rays.

The leader of the herd was an old mare. She decided when it was time to move to another pasture, or travel to a creek to get a drink.

The stallion kept the herd together, and protected it from danger. He always had to be on the alert, and gather the other horses to protect them.

When horses wanted to travel to a different pasture, they walked in a long line together. The stallion was always last. His duty was to make sure that all of the horses in the herd were in front of him and that no horse was left behind.

A horse family

Mare—a female horse

Stallion—a male horse

Gelding—did not exist in the time of wild horses, but we have them nowadays. This is a male horse that has been castrated (has had surgery) so that it can't have any children.

An animal on the alert

The wild horse was an animal of prey, which means that it was an animal that mountain lions and other wild cats hunted and ate. Horses always had to notice any signs of approaching danger so that they could survive. Wild horses were so fast that they could often escape from whatever it was that scared them.

Horses' eyes are on the sides of their face, so they can see what is happening all around them as they graze. Horses have excellent hearing and can move both of their ears separately, which means that they notice many different sounds. If one horse lifts its head and stops to listen, all the other horses in the group stop and listen as well.

A horse has a large range of vision. It can see in many different directions at the same time.

Horses communicate with each other through *body language*; they use their ears, tail, and body position to show what they want to say. They can also make different noises to communicate, like *snorts* and *neighs*.

6

The herd

Horses nowadays are tame, but there are still lots of the wild horse left in them:

- They prefer to be in the company of other horses.
- They scratch each other in places that they can't reach themselves.
- They often stand close together and brush the flies off each other.
- During riding lessons, horses often walk in the same manner that wild horses did—in a long line, one after the other.
- Horses are still cautious around new things. They are curious and often explore objects and people that they aren't familiar with.
- They like to have a good view of their surroundings.

Did you know...

that horses like to be scratched on the withers (the hard top of a horse's shoulders, between the neck and the back)? Horses often scratch each other on and around the withers, and mares do this to their foals (their children) so that they will feel secure and safe.

Horses become tame

People tamed horses for riding, pulling carriages, and carrying heavy objects on their backs.

Before cars were invented, everyone used horses. There were horses all over the world:

- People who lived in the Arabian Desert rode on Arabian horses, which could survive for longer periods of time without water than any other breed.
- American Indians lived together with herds of horses, and their children often learned to ride horses before they learned to walk.
- Cowboys needed horses to help them move their cattle from one pasture to another.
- Soldiers needed horses more than almost anything else. In war, horses carried soldiers on their backs, and they helped transport heavy cannons and other artillery.
- Knights used horses for jousting tournaments, where the knights rode towards each other and tried to knock their opponents off their saddles.
- Farmers plowed, sowed, and harvested their land with the help of horses.

All people in the past rode horses or traveled in a horse-drawn carriage when they wanted to travel long distances.

People needed horses for almost everything that they did!

Did you know that . . .

- the American Indians used to paint their horses before they went to battle? The symbols all had different meanings:
- rings around the eyes gave the horses better vision
- lines over the muzzle and legs showed that the horse was used for battle
- rings around the nostrils gave the horse stamina and patience
- zig zags gave the horse strength and speed
- feathers showed that the horse was unbeatable?

Horses today

Nowadays, we use horses mostly because they are so much fun! Many people have horses who are their best friend and most trusted companion.

In **dressage** (a word that means training), it looks almost as though horses are dancing. They can gracefully move between different gaits (walk, trot, and gallop), and between taking high and long steps.

Jumping horses lift their heads in interest and prick up their ears when they see an obstacle. They love to jump and can make it over obstacles that are both tall and wide.

At a **horse race**, you can watch elegant horses compete against each other. The riders are called *jockeys*, and they are typically small so that the horses can carry as little weight as possible.

At riding schools, you can find **riding ponies and horses**. They are calm, kind, and easy to ride on.

Police use horses to go to places that cars can't go to, such as small streets and in the middle of a crowd of people.

Horses can also be driven in different ways:

A **horse-drawn carriage** is usually used for exhibitions, parades, competitions, or other special occasions like weddings.

In **harness racing**, horses are harnessed to a lightweight cart called a *sulky*. The horse must only trot or pace.

Harnessed work horses are powerful horses that pull plows and heavy carts, or fallen trees from the forest. There is even a lawn mower that horses can pull!

Horses can be big and small

There are many different types of horse breeds, everything from large coldblood horses and slender riding horses to small ponies. The largest horse is the *Shire horse*, which can be up to 18 hands, or around 6 feet tall! Their hooves are about as big as a dinner plate, and their head is very large and long. The smallest is the *miniature horse*, which is only 7 hands, or around 2 and a half feet tall!

Measure a horse's height at its withers. That is why a horse's height is sometimes called the *withers height*. A horse is measured in inches or in *hands*. One hand is 4 inches.

Fifty-eight inches, or 14.2 hands, is an important number. Ponies are shorter than 14.2 hands, and horses are taller than 14.2 hands.

Below is the average withers height for some common horse breeds. Names in italics show the breed's maximum height.

Height (hands)	Breed
20	
19	
18	Shire 17.5 hands
17	Thoroughbred
	Swedish warmblood 16.1 hands
16	Ardennais 15.5 hands
	North Swedish horse, Welsh cob, Lipizzaner, Trotting horse 15.2 hands
14	*Pony, Connemara pony 14.2 hands*
	New Forest, Norwegian Fjord 14 hands
13	*Welsh pony, Icelandic horse 13.5 hands*
	Gotland pony 12.7 hands
	Dartmoor pony 12.5 hands
12	*Welsh Mountain pony 12 hands*
11	
	Shetland pony 10.2 hands
10	
9	
	Miniature Shetland pony 8.4 hands
8	
7	*Miniature horse* 6.9 hands
6	
5	
4	
3	
2	
1	

Did you know...

- that the *Welsh Mountain pony* is often called the most beautiful pony in the world? It has a pretty head, large dark eyes, and small ears. See the photograph to the right.
- that the American breed *Appaloosa* has spots on its body that you can feel with your fingers? The hairs in the spots stand up, but the rest of the hairs on its body lie flat.
- that ponies are smart and full of ideas? They usually learn pretty quickly how to sneak out of the pasture and how to untie the lead rope so that they come loose.

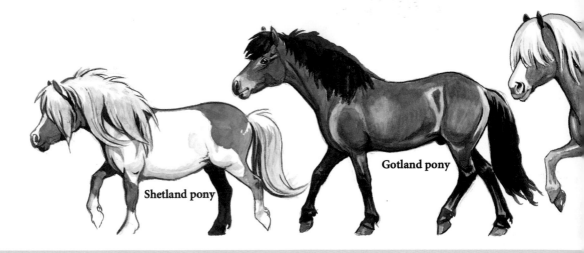

Shetland pony

Gotland pony

Breeds

These are some common breeds:

The *Shetland pony* is one of the smallest ponies in the world. They are friendly, smart, and so strong that they can pull heavy loads, even though they are small.

The *Gotland pony* is a Swedish pony used for riding, harness racing, and driving.

The *Icelandic horse* is often as little as a pony, but is strong enough to carry an adult rider. It has more gaits than other horses, including the tolt, which is an unusual running-walk that is comfortable for the rider.

The *Norwegian Fjord horse* is always a dun color and has a mane that stands straight up. It makes a good horse for a family, as you can ride it and use it for driving.

The *Arabian horse* has a beautiful head, and holds its tail unusually high.

The *North Swedish horse* is a lightweight work horse that is very good at walking on difficult terrain, and at removing fallen trees from a forest. A similar breed is the *North Swedish Trotting horse*, which is often used for racing.

The *Thoroughbred* is used most often in horse racing. They are very beautiful and gentle creatures, and have a thin coat of hair and small, dainty hooves.

The *Tinker horse* comes from Ireland. It is strong, and has a large head and feathering (wispy hairs) on its lower legs and hooves.

Arabian horse

North Swedish horse (also in the photo)

Icelandic horse

Norwegian
Fjord horse

Thoroughbred

Tinker horse

A horse's coat, mane, and tail

The coat

Horses have a thicker coat in the winter, and some breeds grow very long hair. When they shed in the spring, the groomer has quite a job brushing away all that hair! If you groom outside, you'll notice that birds will come by and pick up the loose bits of hair that have fallen on the ground. The birds use the horse hair to make their nests comfortable and cozy for the little baby birds who live there. The outside of some birds' nests are made of the harder strands of horse hair that grow in a horse's mane and tail.

After the horse sheds its hair, it grows a much thinner summer coat. A shiny coat is a sign that a horse is healthy and happy.

A horse's coat smells good; it is a fresh and healthy smell. When horses graze out in the pasture, their coat can also smell like grass.

Bird's nest made with horse hair

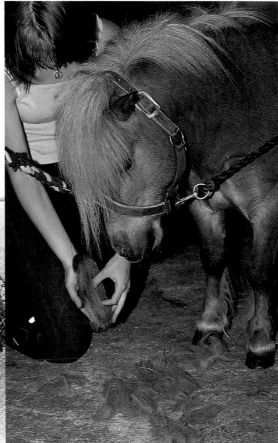

Mane, tail, and forelock

A horse's mane extends from the neck to the withers and can look very different depending on the horse.

Shortened manes are common for Norwegian Fjord horses. Their manes are cut short so their hair stands straight up.

If a mane is shaved off or cut really short, it is called roaching.

Some horse breeds have very long and thick manes.

Did you know that . . .

there are horses with curly coats? The *Russian Bashkir horse* and the *American Curly horse* have curls all over their body, just like poodles. People who are allergic to horses usually have an easier time with curly-haired horses.

Fun horse hairstyles

Before a horse goes to a show it is common to braid its mane. There are lots of different horse hairstyles, and most of these begin with a typical braid.

You need a mane and tail comb, hair clips, hair bands, and a sturdy footstool to stand on when you braid your horse's mane. Here is how you do it:

1. Brush the mane thoroughly.
2. Separate the mane into between 9 and 11 sections, making sure that they are the same size and thickness. Put a hair band on every section.
3. Start by braiding the section that is closest to the neck. Make sure you braid it tightly. Clip the other sections of the mane together so you can work on one braid at a time without the other sections getting in the way.
4. Keep your hands near the horse's throat while you are braiding so that the braids rest on the horse's body instead of sticking straight out.
5. Braid the section all the way down to the bottom, and then tie a hair band at the end.
6. Now you're done! If you want it to be shorter, fold it in half and tie it in place with a hair band.

Practice on yarn, string, or even a friend's hair until you can do beautiful, tight, and even braids!

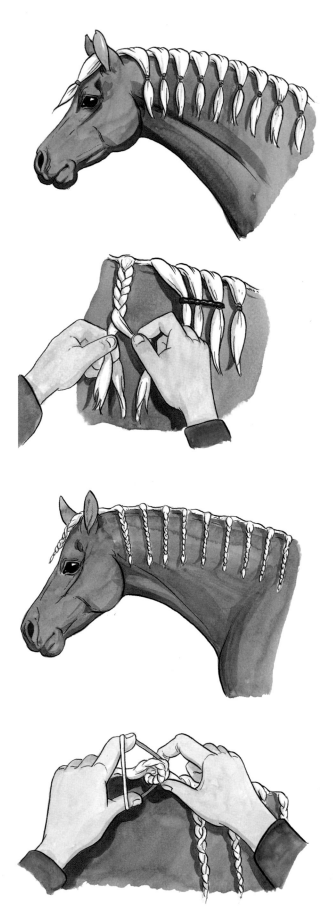

Other types of braids

If you have a horse with a long mane, you can do
one long braid that goes all the way down the crest
(the top part of the horse's neck).

If you have lots of time, you can style a long
mane into a checkered pattern, like the photograph
on the bottom left of the page.

If you have a work horse, you can braid raffia
ribbon into the mane. See picture below.

On special occasions, you can braid beautiful
ribbons of all different colors into the mane. During
the holidays, you can even braid tinsel into your
horse's mane!

French braiding the tail is also fun! You can
collect the loose hair, attach a bow on top, and keep
it so that it will remind you of all the fun times you
and your horse have had together.

How does a horse live?

Horses live in a stable during the cold months of the year. Inside the stable there are stalls and sometimes there is another space where the horses can walk free. The stall is often where the horse stays at night, and it is like a little home.

In order for a horse to be healthy, it needs a stable with a high ceiling and lots of fresh air.

Many stables have an opening to the outside so the horses can stand with their heads outside in the fresh air, and watch what is going on around them. Horses usually enjoy this.

On the floor of the stall is a bed of straw or sawdust for the horses to sleep on. This should be kept clean and dry, so that the horse can lie on something soft and relax when it wants to.

Lots of horses like to have some type of toy to play with in their stall or stable, like a ball or a sturdy brush that hangs from the ceiling.

During the day, the horses are turned out into enclosed pastures or fields, so they can move and be as active as they want. When the weather is nice, they can live like the wild horses did: eat grass, laze around in the sunshine, relax, and take a wonderful gallop with their friends!

Do you know . . .

how to approach a horse when it is in its stall? Since horses are easily scared of things that surprise them, you need to let the horse know you are coming. Make clicking noises with your tongue, or say its name, so that it hears you and turns towards you.

When it turns towards you, calmly walk to the horse and to its head.

HI, TOM!

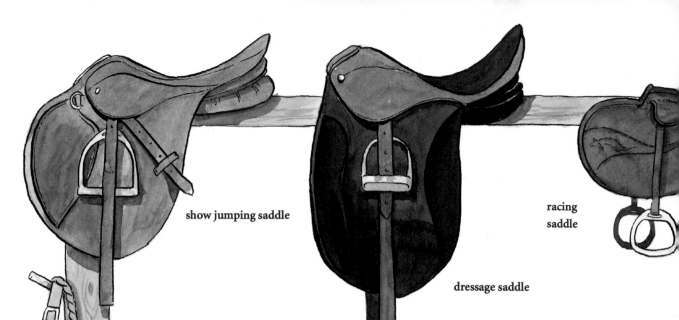

show jumping saddle

racing saddle

dressage saddle

Horse equipment

The most common piece of horse equipment, which is also called tack, is a *halter*. When you lead a horse somewhere, you connect a lead rope to the halter.

The rider sits in a saddle, which comes in many different styles, depending on how you want to ride. Some of the saddle types include dressage saddles, show jumping saddles, western saddles, and saddles made especially for Icelandic horses.

Under the saddle, there is a *saddle pad* (see picture below). It is a blanket that protects the horse's back from chafing and getting sores. The saddle is held in place by a belt called the *girth*.

The rider's feet go in *stirrups*, which give support.

saddle for
Icelandic horses

western saddle

Did you know...

that saddles for race horses are often made in synthetics so that they are as light as possible? A racing saddle can weigh less than a loaf of bread!

Bridles are used to guide the horses. The bridle has reins that are attached to a bit, which the horse has in its mouth. By carefully and gently pulling the reins with your hand, you can get the horse to turn in the direction you want, or to stand still.

Sometimes horses have blankets that they wear when it is rainy or cold. You can find these in many different models, fabrics, and patterns.

When you drive a horse, it has a harness on. There are lots of straps on a harness, and it is important that all of them are in the right place before a cart or anything else is attached to the harness.

Some horses have a mask covering their face during the summer. This protects the horse's face from flies, which can bite and be irritating.

A day in the stable

Julia and Clara each have their own pony: the Dartmoor pony Molasses to the left, and the crossbreed Amanda to the right. We'll follow them into the stable for the day.

Julia and Clara arrive early in the morning, and the ponies welcome them happily with neighs. The ponies are hungry and want some breakfast!

Food pyramid for horses

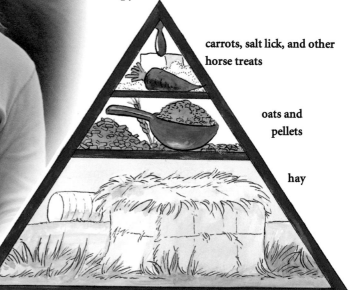

carrots, salt lick, and other horse treats

oats and pellets

hay

Horses have a small stomach and need to eat often.

In the summer, Amanda and Molasses feed on fresh grass, and in the winter they often eat dried grass, which is called hay. Hay and grass make up the biggest part of most horses' diets. They also like to eat oats, carrots, and salt.

Julia gives the horses oats, while Clara carries the hay in to the paddock. The ponies will rest there while the girls are mucking out the stable.

When the ponies have eaten, the girls lead them out into the field. Then they clean up the stable and put all of the manure and wet straw in the wheelbarrow. When the stable and stalls are clean, they put in fresh straw. Fresh hay makes a nice bed for a horse!

The girls wash the horses' water buckets and fill them with fresh water.

Lastly, they sweep the stable floor.

Tip: This is how you make a birthday cake for a horse: take two pieces of crisp bread, put some oats, grass, and carrot slices between the pieces of bread, and place half an apple on top. Yum . . . best birthday cake ever for a horse!

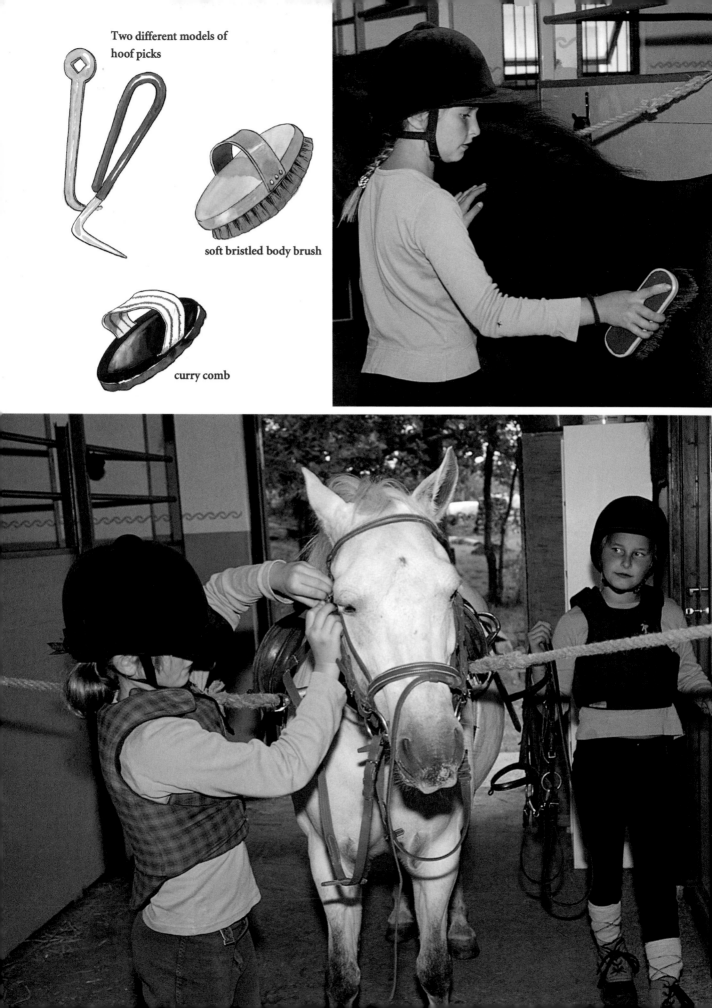

Two different models of hoof picks

soft bristled body brush

curry comb

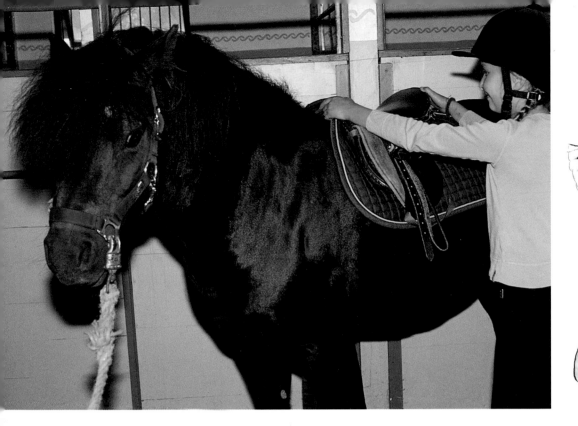

In the afternoon, the girls decide to ride. They take their cleaning buckets, bridles, reins, saddles, and riding helmets, and then go and get their ponies. They tie Molasses and Amanda up in the passage way.

Clara begins by grooming Molasses with a *dandy brush*. This brush, which has stiff, long bristles, is used to remove the patches of dirt. Then she uses a *soft bristled body brush* and grooms the whole horse using long strokes across the horse's body. Every few strokes, she cleans the brush with a *curry comb*. The grayish-white dust that collects on the curry comb is part of the horse's skin that has been removed by the grooming process. The curry comb also needs to be cleaned.

The mane and tail are brushed using a brush with stiffer bristles, or a special mane and tail comb. The hooves are cleaned with a *hoof pick*.

When she is done grooming Molasses, Clara saddles him up. She places the saddle high up towards his mane, and then carefully brings it back until it is in the right place. This way his hair is flat under the saddle and doesn't chafe him. Then she tightens and secures the girth, so the saddle is firmly in place.

Now it is time for the bridle. Amanda is nice and opens her mouth and receives the bit so that Julia can place the headstall over her ears and secure the noseband and throatlatch.

The girls have put on their riding helmets and vests. Now they are ready to ride!

They enjoy a long and exciting ride, where they walk, trot, and gallop on soft forest paths. Sometimes they ride their ponies in an arena, so they can learn to follow directions and move more gracefully. Sometimes they also practice jumping over obstacles. Once a week they train with a riding instructor.

One of the best things about riding horses is that no matter how good you are, there is more to learn. You can always discover something new! Before Amanda and Molasses return to the stable, they are allowed to cool down and walk around with the girls still on their backs.

After riding, Clara and Julia take off the saddles and brush the horses. They also wipe off any moisture until the horses are completely dry and the hair on their coats is flat. In their stalls, the horses have water to drink and hay to eat.

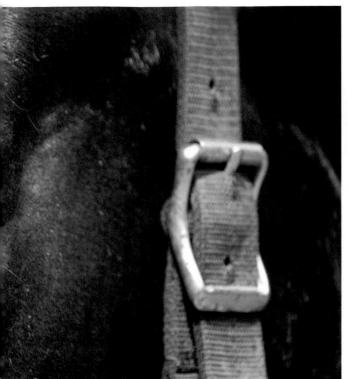

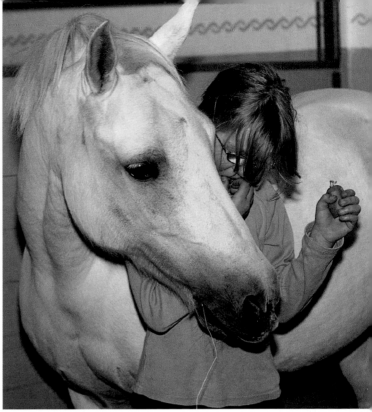

Now it is time for a break. The girls sit down and enjoy a delicious snack. A sandwich, juice, and an apple taste fantastic after riding and being in the stable for several hours! The ponies can smell the apples and want a little taste of their own.

Full and content, the girls gather some soap for the saddle, water, and a sponge. They clean the saddle and bridle (the leather should be soft and comfortable), and then hang them up in the right place.

Before it is time for them to cycle home, they refill the horses' water and give them their dinner: oats and a large portion of hay that should last through the night. The only thing left is the good night hug, and Julia and Clara leave the stable to go back home to their families.

The farrier visits!

frost nails

A horse's feet, *hooves*, have a hard layer of skin on the outside. This helps protect the foot's *sole*, which is sensitive. It is very important to take good care of a horse's hooves, because without them the horse cannot move properly. Before you ride, you should always check that no rocks have gotten stuck to the hooves, which can hurt the soles. Clean all of the dirt and pebbles away with a hoof pick.

It is exciting when the farrier comes to the stable! He *trims* the hooves when they get too long. This means that he shortens the hooves using a hammer and a rasp file.

Some horses need shoes, which help to prevent injuries by protecting the most vulnerable parts of their hooves. The horseshoes are attached to the hoof with *horseshoe nails*. The horseshoe nails are nailed to the hoof in places where the horse has no feeling, so it doesn't hurt the horse.

Sometimes the farrier attaches *studs* to the horseshoes, which prevent horses from slipping on wet grass, snow, and ice.

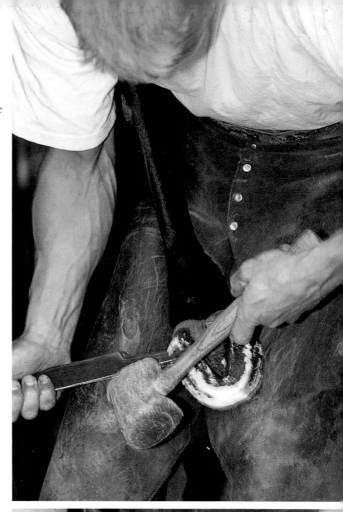

horseshoe nails

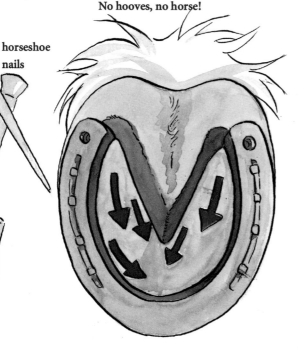

No hooves, no horse!

Clean the hoof in the direction of the arrows.

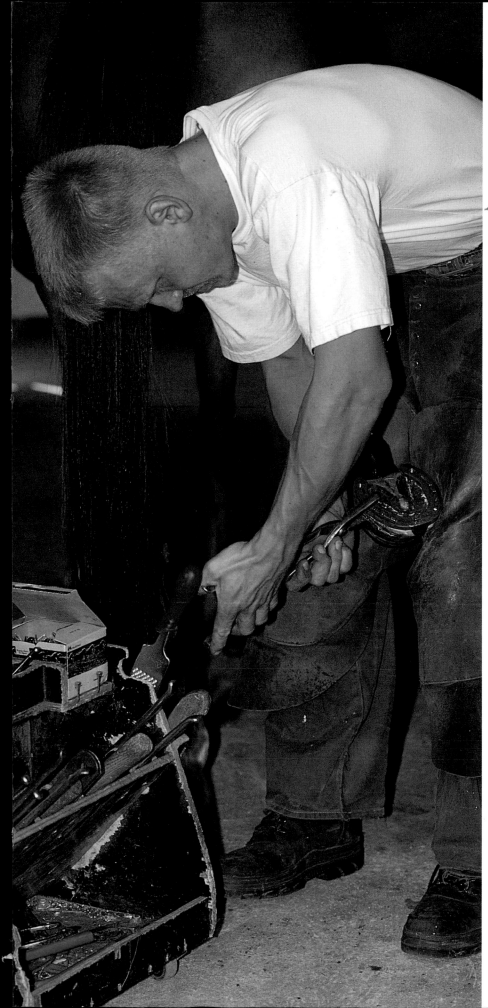

Did you know...

... that a horseshoe above a door means good luck? But it has to be turned with the ends up, otherwise the luck will run out!

... that you can make new objects out of old horseshoes? Candlesticks, seesaw handles, bars for the stalls, hooks to hang things on, and photo frames are just some of the fun things that you can make.

A horse's relatives and four-legged friends

Donkeys and zebras are cousins to the horse. They have hooves and are similar to horses, but there are also many differences between them. Both donkeys and zebras have a firm tail, which has horse hair only at the very bottom.

Donkeys are gray or brown, and have long ears. They are very patient and strong, and are often used to pull wagons or carts, or to carry loads on their backs. They can walk along very narrow and steep paths in the mountains, where no cars can go.

If you have ever heard a donkey yell, it is something that you will never forget! It is a high and shrill sound.

A zebra's ears are not as long as a donkey's ears, but they are still a little bit longer than horse ears. The mane is short and stands straight up. The entire body of a zebra is striped and either black and white, or brown and white. No two zebras have the exact same pattern of stripes on their bodies.

A zebra doesn't sound like a horse or a donkey. It has more of a barking sound.

Zebras are rarely tame, as most of them are wild and live in herds in Africa.

Friends of the horse

Horses prefer to be friends with other horses, but they can also make friends with other animals. Some of a horse's friends can be rabbits, goats, dogs, and cats.

I want to ride!

The day will soon come when you will want to ride a horse. When you sit on a horse, you will feel how its body moves gracefully beneath you, hear the sound of the saddle creaking, and realize that you can actually get a large horse to go where you want it to go.

The first few times you ride, you will probably be riding with a friend or will go on a short pony ride. If you enjoy being with horses and feel that it is something you really want to do, then you also have to learn how to communicate with them and take care of them properly. You can learn how to do all of this at a riding school. Many riding schools require that you are at least seven years old, but there are some that let younger kids ride, too.

Try to find a riding school where you not only get a chance to ride, but also learn how to take care of horses in the best way possible.

34

Remember that . . .

the calm horses at riding school are used to beginners. If you ride somewhere else, you are going to meet horses that are more lively and sensitive. These horses often react much more quickly than horses at riding schools.

Durable clothes

You don't need to have special riding clothes when you start riding. The most important thing is that your clothes are durable and warm, because it can get very cold in the stable.

Wear pants that don't have big seams on the inside, and boots or thick shoes with solid soles and heels. Sneakers are too soft to ride in. You can borrow a helmet at the riding school.

After you've decided that you want to continue, you can buy riding clothes. Start with comfortable riding pants, a helmet, and gloves. Later on you can add riding boots and a vest.

The first lesson

Almost everyone has butterflies in their stomach when they take their first riding lesson. How is it going to go? Is the horse going to be kind and calm?

A riding teacher makes sure that you are going to get a horse that works well for you. The children who have ridden the least get the safest and nicest horses.

The more time you spend with horses, the more you start to think about them. You even start to see horses everywhere!

You don't have to ride . . . driving is also fun! You can learn by taking driving lessons. In the beginner's course, you learn about horse grooming, how to harness a horse, and how to hold the reins. In the beginning, there are always two people sitting in the cart. The more you learn, the more you get to drive. After you have been to lessons for a while, you will get to drive alone, and very fast if you want to!

Many talented drivers started by taking driving lessons at riding schools.

Horseback riding camp can be the ultimate dream for anyone who loves horses! There, you have your own horse for an entire week. You can go into the field and spend time with the horses first thing in the morning, and after dinner in the evening. You also get to go on long rides through the forest, ride bareback (no saddle), and learn everything you need to know about taking care of a horse.

Before you go to a horseback riding camp, you should have some experience riding and going to riding school, because at camp you'll do lots of riding!

Many people enjoy their camp so much that they go back to the same one every year.

Leave your grooming kit at home!

Do you ride at home or take care of horses in another stable? Maybe you have your own grooming supplies, including brushes, a hoof pick, and a sponge? Make sure you always ask the owner of the horse if you can use your own grooming kit. You can spread infectious diseases from one horse to another if you use your own grooming kit on more than one horse. Most horses have their own grooming supplies, which are used only on that horse.

Horse Jumping!

Have you ever dreamt about being able to jump a real course, with all different types of obstacles? Below are some of the common show jumping obstacles. The flags show which direction you should be coming from when you jump: if the white flag is on your left and the red flag is on your right, then you know that you are jumping from the right direction.

The horse and rider team that finishes a course with the least number of faults (the word for penalty points) is the winner.

The diagram on the next page tells you the order of the obstacles (begin with number 1).

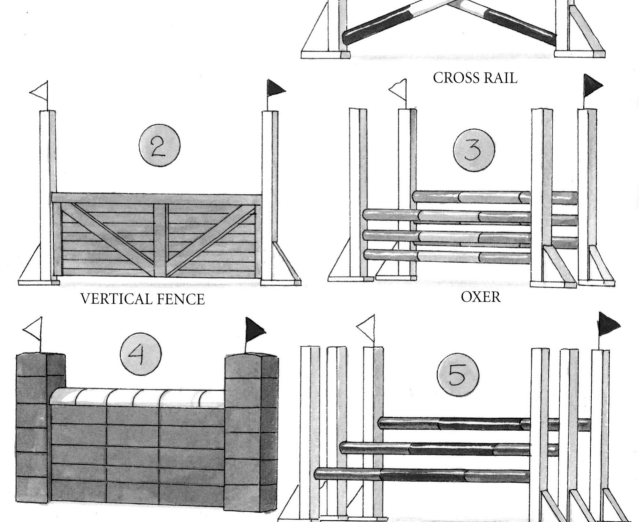

CROSS RAIL

VERTICAL FENCE

OXER

WALL

TRIPLE BAR

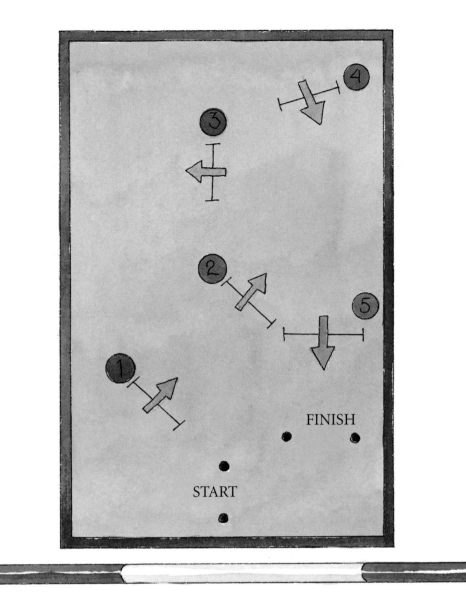

Faults

Knocking down obstacle = 4 faults

Refusal = 4 faults

If you or the horse falls = disqualified

GOOD LUCK!

Your own horse collection!

Most people who like horses want to have some horse collectibles of their own. They collect pictures, mugs, plates, and other objects that have horses on them.

You can also collect photos, postcards, bookmarks, or stamps with horses on them, and make an album. Every time you look in your album, you can daydream a little . . . pretend they are all your horses and give them cute names.

Make your own toy horse!

Tons of fun can be had with a toy horse! Ask an adult for help:

1. Draw a horse's head in profile and two ears on a piece of cloth that has been folded in half.
2. Cut the pattern out, leaving an inch around the edges for when you sew it. Leave six inches of fabric below the neck.
3. Sew the two pieces together while the cloth is inside out. Leave an opening for the neck.
4. Turn the head right side out, and sew on the ears.
5. Fill the head and ears with stuffing.
6. Put a dowel or a stick in the neck. Make sure you pack the head and ears tight. Sew the opening around the dowel by hand. Tie the fabric below the neck to the dowel with rubber bands.
7. Draw on the eyes and nostrils with a felt tip pen. Sew on some pieces of yarn for the mane.
8. The bridle and reins can be made of ribbon, braided yarn, or rope.
9. Now your toy horse is ready!

Bareback

Horse dictionary

age – You can tell a horse's age by looking at his teeth, which grow as he grows older. Ask someone to show you how.

arena – a fenced ring or corral in which people ride horses.

back – to move a horse to the rear. Sometimes called rein-back.

bareback – to ride a horse without a saddle.

bay – a horse with a brown coat and black mane and tail.

bit – the metal object in the horse's mouth to which the reins are attached.

blaze – a white mark down a horse's face. See page 45 for this and other facial markings.

breaking in, or gentling – teaching a young horse to be comfortable when being ridden or driven.

Chestnut

breed – a group of horses or ponies that all have the same appearance. Thoroughbreds, Quarter Horses, and Shetland Ponies are examples of breeds.

bridle – the leather straps that go over the horse's head to hold the bit.

canter – a three-beat gait; a slow gallop.

cantle – the rear of a saddle.

cavaletti – low obstacles for horses to jump. The word is Italian for "little horses."

chaps – leather coverings that go over the rider's pant legs to support and protect the legs.

chestnut – a horse with a light brown coat, mane, and tail. Also called sorrel.

clip – to trim the horse's body and leg hair.

Chaps

Points

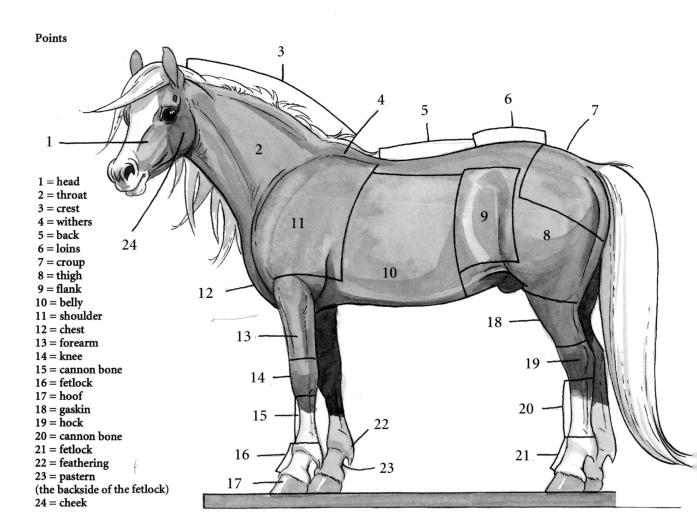

1 = head
2 = throat
3 = crest
4 = withers
5 = back
6 = loins
7 = croup
8 = thigh
9 = flank
10 = belly
11 = shoulder
12 = chest
13 = forearm
14 = knee
15 = cannon bone
16 = fetlock
17 = hoof
18 = gaskin
19 = hock
20 = cannon bone
21 = fetlock
22 = feathering
23 = pastern
(the backside of the fetlock)
24 = cheek

Gymkhana

colic – a stomach ache that often comes from a horse's eating too much or eating the wrong food.

colt – a male horse under the age of four years.

crop – a short stick used to encourage a horse to move forward.

curb – the long-shanked bit that most western horses wear.

diagonal – the rider's posting movement in relation to the horse's trot steps. A rider who posts up when the horse's left foreleg is off the ground is said to be on left diagonal.

feathers – the long hair on the back of the lower legs of certain breeds.

fetlock – the joint right above the feet.

filly – a female horse under the age of four years.

foal – a baby horse under the age of one year.

fore leg – either of the horse's front legs.

free jumping (or loose jumping) – a horse jumping down a chute or around an arena without a rider on its back.

girth – the strap that goes under the horse's belly to hold the saddle in place.

gallop – a horse's fastest gait.

gait – the way a horse moves its legs, such as the walk, trot, canter, and gallop.

gray – a horse with mostly white and some dark-colored hair.

gymkhana – a program of games on horseback.

halt – to stop a horse.

head shy – a horse that doesn't like its head touched.

hind leg – either of the horse's back legs.

lope – the western word for canter.

longe (pronounced "lunge") – to exercise a horse moving around a person who holds a long line attached to the horse's halter.

Unusual facial markings

44

mare – a female horse aged four years or older.

martingale – a strap that runs from the girth between the horse's legs to the bridle. It helps to keep a horse's head down.

mount – to get on a horse.

mounting block – a step that makes getting on a horse easier.

near side – the horse's left side.

noseband – the part of the bridle that goes over the horse's nose.

off side – the horse's right side.

oxer – a wide jump.

paddock – a small fenced area where horses can move around as they wish.

pace – a gait in which the horse's legs on the same side move together.

Paint – a breed that has patches of white or another color on their bodies. A horse that is marked that way but is not a member of the Paint breed is called a Pinto.

points – the outside parts of the horse's body. See page 43.

pommel – the front of a saddle.

post – to move up and down as the horse trots to make the trot more comfortable to ride. Also called rising trot.

Horse show ribbons

blaze

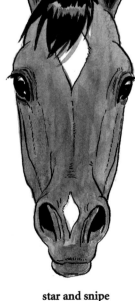

star and snipe

stripe

Gray mare with chestnut foal

Quarter Horse – a breed developed to herd cattle in the American West.

rear – to stand up on the hind legs, a very dangerous habit.

refuse – to stop in front of a jump.

reins – the leather straps attached to the bridle that the rider or driver holds.

rosette – the ribbon that horse show prize-winners are awarded.

Riding reins

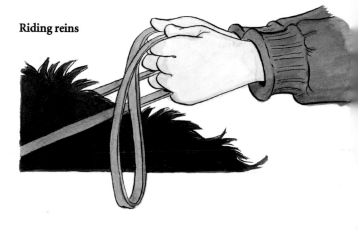

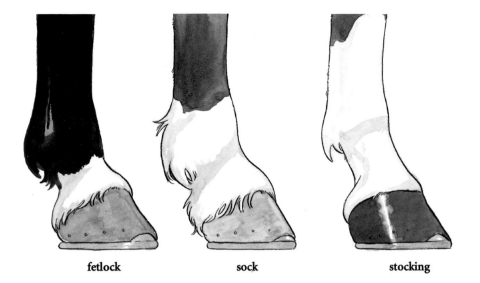

fetlock   sock   stocking

side-saddle – a kind of riding in which women sit on
    a special saddle that allows them to keep both
    legs on the horse's left side.
spurs – metal objects worn on the rider's boots to
    encourage the horse to move forward.
trot – a four-beat gait in which the horse's diagonal
    legs move together.
walk – the horse's slowest gait.
western saddle – a saddle used by cowboys and
    other western-style riders.

Pinto

Skyhorse Publishing books may be purchased in bulk at special discounts for sales promotion, corporate gifts, fund-raising, or educational purposes. Special editions can also be created to specifications. For details, contact the Special Sales Department, Skyhorse Publishing, 555 Eighth Avenue, Suite 903, New York, NY 10018 or info@skyhorsepublishing.com.

www.skyhorsepublishing.com

10 9 8 7 6 5 4 3 2 1

Library of Congress Cataloging-in-Publication Data

Andersson, Ingrid.
   My first book of horses / by Ingrid Andersson ; illustrated by Lena Furberg ; photographs by Marie Paulsson-Bertmar.
      p. cm.
   ISBN 978-1-61608-033-4 (hardcover : alk. paper)
   1. Horses. I. Title.
   SF285.A637 2010
   636.1--dc22
                                      2010001771

Printed in China